CONFIDENTLY PRICE YOUR WORK

Kelsey,

I'm so proud of you + all your accomplishments! Thank you for all your support + love!

"For the Dreamers"

Copyright © 2022 by Kerry Lofton

All rights reserved.

No part of this book may be reproduced in any form or by any electronic or mechanical means, including information storage and retrieval systems, without written permission from the author, except for the use of brief quotations in a book review.

CONTENTS

Acknowledgments	vii
Introduction	xv
1. Know Your Worth	1
2. It Takes Money To Make Money	22
3. It's Not What You Sell, It's How You Sell It	32
4. You Gotta Be Willing To Negotiate	46
5. What You Do With It Is Up To You	60
6. Free Game	63
One Step back, Two steps forward	65
Always Have Contracts In Place	67
Jack of All Trades, Master of None	69
Charge Late Fees	71
Get Half of Ya' Bread Upfront	73
Underpromise and Overdeliver	75
Everybody Eats	77
Tiered Pricing	79
You Don't Need A New Camera	81
Take Breaks Often	83
Say No…A Lot	85
Take 'Em To Court	87
When They Go Left, You Go Up	89
Extra resources	91
About the Author	93

ACKNOWLEDGEMENTS

First and foremost, thank you to my Lord and Savior, Jesus Christ. Without the gifts and talents You have blessed me with, I couldn't snap a photo, edit a video, or write a word. May all the glory and praise for the wisdom in this book be directed to You alone!

To my beautiful wife Bri - I'm so thankful for you and the light you bring to my life. This book might not have ever come to fruition without you by my side. Thank you for being so supportive every step of the way. Thank you for being okay with my long trips to coffee shops to write. Thank you for listening to countless chapter revisions, encouraging me every time I wanted to give up, and being my biggest inspiration to pursue God's will for my life. Most of all, thank you for praying for me so much. I know I'm so covered every day because you are constantly petitioning on my behalf. I love you!

To my family, thank you for your support in all that I do. It truly means the world!

Rishunn - Thank you for not only changing my life physically as my trainer, but also spiritually and mentally through the conversations we have, many of which inspired this book. Every day I walk into that gym I'm becoming stronger in more ways than one. I'm truly thankful for our friendship!

And to all the people I could never name one by one, thank you! The support of so many, some I know personally and others I don't, means so much.

This is for everyone like me. The ones who got it out of the mud with no Harvard business degree. You might be figuring it out as you go, but you're making it happen. I'm proud of you! I'm proud of us!

THIS STUFF WORKS

"Kerry has always been super helpful and willing to share with creatives. He's a rare breed. I recently transitioned to a full-time entrepreneur, owning a creative production agency. Going from being just a graphic designer to now running operations, budgeting and everything that involves running a business was a big transition for me. Black creatives as a whole are severely underpaid and undervalued. Kerry walked me through rates and the things I would've never even thought to charge for!"

— *Jas Alston*
Founder and Creative Director, The BLK Originals

"Kerry has been the best teammate and most creative person I've ever worked with. He is also my go-to to ask for professional advice, providing intelligible, honest, and insightful information with every conversation. I'm grateful to have met him through work and to have him as an influential friend in my life."

— *Dana Byrnes*
Digital Content and Social Strategy Manager, Roc Nation Sports

"Kerry has a wealth of information when it comes to knowing your worth as a creative. He opened my eyes and changed my perspective on how I should be billing clients for my time. Our time is valuable and should be properly paid for, and should include everything we spend time doing for the project, including but not limited to meetings, research, setup, filming, editing, and revisions. He reminded me that at the end of the day, when people value you and your work, they won't question the price on the invoice because you're worth it."

— *Tamara Brown*
Host and Content Producer, New England Patriots

"For years I have struggled with knowing my worth as a professional photographer. Working with Kerry on projects has pushed me to not be afraid to charge my worth. He has taught me that I must compensate myself for every task I do in my line of work. I went from charging hourly rates per shoot to day rates and booking larger projects. If you're dreaming about making a move in your career as a creative, this book has all of the answers to your questions."

— *Adriana Herrera*
Photographer and Entrepreneur

"From training Kerry 3x weekly, the insight and knowledge he was bringing is worth millions. In our random conversations, Kerry taught me the true meaning of knowing your value first. From setting up a budget list, to teaching me about tithing, Kerry helped me in tons of ways that I'm beyond grateful for. The biggest thing was one hundred percent knowing how to set your price based on the value you bring and owning it with confidence. As I was helping him physically he was helping me financially and mentally as well."

— Rishunn McCaleb
Personal Coach, Faith Street Fitness

"Kerry truly has a heart for creatives, especially new ones like myself who had no idea how to navigate the waters of freelancing and pricing their work. Not only did he give me practical advice, but he provided tangible examples for me to value my work and my time."

— Miracle Pearsall
Freelance Graphic Designer

THERE'S A LOT OF GRAY AREA WHEN IT COMES TO PRICING. NO TWO PROJECTS ARE EVER THE SAME AND 1+1 DOESNT ALWAYS EQUAL 2.

IT CAN BE SCARY AND CONFUSING, BUT YOU CAN BE PREPARED TO FACE IT.

INTRODUCTION

WHY IS IT SO COMPLICATED?

- "How much do you charge for your services?"
- "Do you have a menu or a rate sheet?"
- "I don't have a budget for this project. Can you just give me a price?"

If you experienced a little bit of anxiety reading those sentences, you're probably like most people who hate having to discuss money. Talking about pricing is one of the most dreaded conversations we have with clients. Creating? That's the easy part. Dealing with the numbers? That's a bit more complicated! That's what stresses most of us out.

It's like in the *Lion King*, when Mufasa told Simba "Nah, son, we don't go there." We avoid thinking and talking about money like the elephant boneyard. Similar to others, I've dealt with the stress and anxiety of pricing in my own video production business. The whole concept seems overwhelming and frustrating, but as we'll see, it doesn't have to be that way.

THE GREAT UNKNOWN

There is one place you will never find me: on a cruise ship. Cruising seems to be an incredibly fun way to travel for some people, but I could not imagine enjoying it myself.

I'm not afraid that the ship will sink or that I'll get seasick. I avoid cruises because being in the middle of the ocean at night sounds absolutely terrifying. Just thinking about looking out and seeing nothing but darkness for miles gives me the creeps. And don't even get me started on my theories about sea monsters. That could probably be a whole other book.

My apprehension for getting on cruise ships is, in a way, the same reason so many creatives and business owners fear talking about money and pricing—the great unknown. They don't know what's out there or how to start searching for the right answers. The minute someone asks them to give a price for their work, their mind becomes as dark and blank as the ocean in the middle of the night.

"How much is too much, and how little is too little?" This mental tug-of-war goes on with every new project. Moreover, a lack of confidence causes many people to severely undervalue themselves. I've rarely seen anyone who lacks confidence overestimate their value. To paraphrase Michelangelo's famous quote, "We would rather aim low and hit our mark than aim high and miss."

SEARCHING FOR AN ANSWER THAT DOESN'T EXIST

I'm very vocal and transparent about my own pricing journey on social media. Because of this, creatives and business owners started reaching out to me for help with their prices. That influx of people seeking my advice was why I decided to write this book. I was at the point where I was having money conversations with my peers four to five times a week!

However, I found that many of them were searching for something I could not give: the golden number. Maybe you picked up this book expecting the same answer as well. Unfortunately, I have to tell you the same thing I often tell those asking for my help: there is no "right" answer. Before you toss this book in the trash, let me explain.

There is no absolute value in this world. You can only estimate what a thing is worth to you. Although I can offer advice, I cannot set anyone's prices for them. I can rarely say, "Yeah, you should be charging X amount."

When it comes to pricing different types of work, especially creative work, there is a lot of gray area. Each project is unique, and 1+1 doesn't always equal 2. Things like experience, skill set, equipment, licensing, and even geographical location can play a part in what the final number can end up being. So while I could never walk through all of those variables with someone, there is a process I can show them to arrive at the number they are seeking.

MATH SUCKS, BUT I'M USING IT AS AN EXAMPLE

Back in high school, I used to tell people that my favorite subject was history, and math was my least favorite. History was easy because all I had to do was memorize everything. The information doesn't change. The answer to the question, "When did World War I begin?" is always 1914.

But math is more challenging. You can learn the formulas and processes, but the answers on the test will always be different because the problems will be different. You can learn the principles of addition to know that 2+2=4, but that doesn't mean you'll walk into the test, and the first question will be, "What is 2+2?" You're walking into the test with knowledge of the process, not a specific final answer.

Just like with math, you may not start out with the right answer, but you can have a formula and a plan to find the right price to set for your work. As a result of much trial and error, talking to people in different fields, asking questions, and researching, I have found a system that works for me, and I believe it can work for you.

Using the information in this book, you will be able to clear up some of the confusion, learn what questions to ask, and how to approach setting your price for various situations and jobs. The details of a project can change, but the rules and principles remain the same.

Now, here's the disclaimer: This isn't a magic trick to get rich. I didn't write this book to help you fatten your pockets. Could that happen as you apply the information? Absolutely! I pray that your business and work prospers beyond your wildest dreams! But there are things far more important than money at stake.

I cannot promise that all proposals will be accepted, your job will double your salary, you won't have to negotiate anymore, or you won't have to think about it extensively. Practice is required, and as you get more experience in business, you will face a lot of unique challenges.

Though I've gotten more comfortable with the process, there are still times when I have to sit down, use my brain, and work the numbers. However, I'm stepping into those situations with the confidence that I've done everything to be prepared.

And what I can promise you is that when you apply the information provided in this book, you will have the tools to walk with that same level of confidence. This mindset that I use in my daily business dealings allows me to consistently work with high-budget clients and present my price confidently.

These principles helped me learn how to understand and communicate the true worth and value of my work and are the very ideas that helped me grow my production company to over six figures in under a year with still an upwards trend.

This book isn't just for creatives either! Entrepreneurs, freelancers, and even people working salaried jobs can benefit from knowing their value, applying the right formulas, and confidently putting a number on their work.

Now, without further ado, let's begin. Since this is

essential information, this book is short and sweet. The world already has a lot of textbooks, so I didn't want to create another. The chapters are organized in the order in which I go through my own process of setting my prices.

We'll start with learning how to put a value on ourselves and understand our worth. In chapter two, we'll cover how to get a return on the investments we make into our businesses. Chapter three covers how to create professional proposals and budgets and confidently present them to clients. And finally, in chapter four, we go over the proper context for negotiations and discounts.

The quicker you finish this book and digest the information, the sooner you will be able to get out and start receiving your full worth. Are you ready?

CHAPTER 1

KNOW YOUR WORTH

> *You don't get paid for the hour. You get paid for the value you bring to the hour.*
>
> Jim Rohn, Entrepreneur

Before we can go any further, we need to do a little bit of housekeeping. I need you to remove any negative thoughts you may have about yourself and your work. Some of you may already have this in order but still join in this exercise with me. Read the following out loud to yourself:

"I am valuable. I am worthy. I deserve to profit off of the skills and talents I have been blessed with. My gifts are designed to make room for me. I belong here. I have nothing to lose, and nothing to prove."

Do you believe that? If you don't, go back and reread it. Keep rereading it until it is tattooed on your brain. This lie has infiltrated so many people's minds that repeating the quote several times may not undo the damage caused by a long history of toxic thinking. Some of you may be so deep into insecurity and self-doubt that there's no way you can believe those statements right now. Whatever you have to do to rid yourself of this mindset, I encourage you to make that your first priority. Without understanding this fundamental truth, everything else in the book will be useless to you; it will be like pouring water into a bottomless cup.

This isn't some mantra-repeating gimmick, either. I'm not expecting you to magically think yourself confident, nor do I plan on giving you the seven secret steps to happiness. I'm trying to get you to build the foundation necessary to reach your full potential. Without a proper foundation, no matter how beautiful a house may look on the inside and out, it will be flawed at its core and eventually crumble.

Though the phrase "Know your worth" has been reduced to an overly used cliché, it is the key to everything I plan on discussing in this book. You need to get this! Otherwise, you'll just convince yourself that it's good information, but it can never work for you.

IMPOSTER SYNDROME

Social media has masked the effects of it, but imposter syndrome is running rampant in our society. For those unfamiliar with the term, it was introduced by psychologists Suzanna Imes and Pauline Rose Clance in the 1970s.[1] Imposter syndrome is defined as "the feeling that you don't measure up, that you are not deserving of high esteem or success, and that everything you've achieved was out of luck and not skill and talent." Many people call it "the silent career killer" because it sneaks in through the backdoor disguised as humility and causes the person struggling with it to discount every one of their achievements and accolades. They want to believe that they are worthy, and every post on Instagram tries to reflect that, but deep inside, people are struggling to accept the true value of themselves and their work.

Here's a simple test to know if you may be struggling with imposter syndrome. If someone asks for your price and you're thinking about what to charge, do you land on a number and then immediately start trying to lower it or think of reasons why it may be too high?

How about when you do get a project and you charge full price, do you feel guilty about it when you receive the money? Like you don't deserve it?

When someone applauds your work, do you lean into the compliment and accept it or do you brush it off and think that person is just being nice?

If you said yes to any of those questions, you may be struggling with imposter syndrome.

Don't be discouraged, though; you're not the only person dealing with it. Even the people with the best-looking lives on social media can be struggling with it behind closed doors.

I remember fighting off imposter syndrome when I won my first Lonestar Emmy. Although that award was a fantastic accomplishment for my career, it soon caused me to spiral into a cycle of depression and anxiety. I felt like I didn't really deserve it at the time. To add to the weight of it all, I started to have this pressure to perform. I felt like I couldn't afford to put bad work out anymore.

Every video had to be flawless, or I felt like I wasn't measuring up.

I even experienced imposter syndrome while writing this book. I almost scrapped this whole project at least ten times. I'd lie awake in bed many nights thinking, *Nobody wants to hear what you have to say. What makes you so special, and who gave you any authority to speak on this? Someone out there who knows more than you is going to call you an idiot.*

It should have been easy to shut those thoughts up because I have evidence that they are false. I can look around and see that my work is deserving of an Emmy. I can look at the financials of my business and see that the information in this book is working. But when our minds tell us that we aren't worth anything, why is it so hard to ignore?

There's a quote that says, "If someone else spoke to you the way you speak to yourself, would you be friends with them?"

It can feel impossible to shut off the engine of your negative thoughts about yourself once it gets going, but it is crucial to your success. You can never expect the world to see and honor your actual value if you don't first do it yourself.

YOUR MIND IS MESSING WITH YOUR MONEY

Imposter syndrome affects more than just mental health. Financially, it can harm you as well.

A study done by the research company Jobvite found

that only twenty-nine percent of job seekers were negotiating their salary.[2] More than half of the population in this country merely accepts what is being given to them without a fight. And before we assume that money isn't being left on the table, that same study says that eighty-four percent of those who asked for more money received it. When surveyed as to why workers weren't negotiating higher salaries, fear and a lack of self-confidence were among the top answers.

As creatives, we love to scream from the mountaintops about bad clients who don't want to pay us. I see it on social media all the time; someone talking about how they didn't get paid or how a company was being so cheap. We all probably have a terrible money story we can share, so I'm not attacking the validity of these experiences. There are definitely some disrespectfully cheap people out there.

But the proof is in the numbers that the burden mainly lies with us. A lot of times, we have not because we ask not. We discount ourselves before giving the client a chance to do so.

CLOSED MOUTHS DON'T GET FED

If you're waiting on your clients to pay you more out of the kindness of their hearts or for your job to hand you the raise you think you deserve, I have some bad news for you: It won't happen. The task of putting a value on yourself is one that only you can complete. But even though this is our responsibility, we're sometimes too eager to pass it off to others. And you can't expect someone to put the proper value on something that doesn't belong to them.

It's like when Tony Stark gave Peter Parker those Stark Industries glasses in *Spider-Man: Far from Home*. Instead of accepting the honor of becoming the next Iron Man, Peter passed them off to Mysterio, who had bad intentions. And because the glasses or the responsibility didn't originally belong to Mysterio, he was careless with how he handled them, and chaos ensued.

What about you? You may not have Iron Man's glasses, but you hold in your possession something important. You get to decide the price you put on yourself and your services. Who are you allowing to set your value? If you say anybody other than yourself, the answer is wrong.

WE ALL LOVE A GOOD DEAL

Don't take it personally when clients or companies don't know how to correctly place value on you or your work. It's human nature for people to always look for the best deal available. It's not about you; it's about the innate human desire to discount everything. Let me give you an example to prove that theory.

Imagine yourself walking into a Lamborghini dealership. You have five hundred thousand dollars in a duffle bag, prepared to buy your dream car. You don't need to negotiate or ask for any financing. You've researched it, know how much it costs down to the penny, you've saved, and you're ready to buy. You greet the sales associate, point out the one you want, and they tell you, "You're in luck! Today we're allowing customers to decide how much this car is worth to them and pay what they want."

What do you think you'll do in that situation? If you say that you would still put five hundred thousand dollars on the table, you need to repent for lying. Anybody in their right mind would say the lowest number possible. Why? Because we still try to get a deal, even when things are valuable to us. Psychology studies have shown that humans seem to be wired for chasing down a good deal.

For some clients, it's not about anything other than the thrill they get from negotiating. Don't take it personally; take control. You can choose to stand on your price and be confident about the number you are presenting.

But how do you even know what's fair and what's not? How do you arrive at that number? For a person who says they hate math, I'm about to ask you to do some.

HOW TO FIND YOUR WORTH

As I started to figure out the best way to set and communicate my prices, the first thing I had to determine was how much I wanted to charge for myself. This meant that I had to find a way to place a numerical value on the skills I possess, my time, and the expertise I was bringing to any project. Everything you do in pricing yourself revolves around two things:

- The unique skills you have cultivated and your professional experience
- Your level of ability to perform the task requested, i.e., how quickly and efficiently you can get the job done and deliver results.

Understanding those two things, the easiest way to put it all into perspective is to use the following equation:

$$Experience + Performance = Worth.$$

You might be thinking, *Hold up, that equation can't give me the number I'm looking for. There aren't even any numbers in it. No wonder this guy hates math; he's terrible at it!*

Don't worry. We'll get to the process of finding actual numbers, I promise. But before we can, you have to understand how to look at those numbers and apply them to your own situation.

YOU WORKED HARD FOR YOUR RÉSUMÉ, LET IT WORK HARD FOR YOU

The first thing that affects the numbers you'll be looking at is your professional experience. The places you've been and your skills are unique to you. This is especially true in creative work. Even though you may be one photographer out of a million other photographers, there is only one you. There may be others who can do the job, but they cannot do it the same way. They may be just as talented and capable, but that still does not mean you are the same.

That also goes for graphic designers, videographers, writers, musicians, artists, hairstylists, personal trainers, chefs, etc. Just because you operate in a field where others do the same thing as you doesn't mean that you are bringing the same thing to the table as someone else.

You mustn't downplay your skills or experience. Remember, resist the urge to aim low. We work hard to attain specific skills and hone our craft. We spend hours learning, reading, watching YouTube and tutorials, listening to podcasts, and doing whatever else to be at the top of our fields. You need to make sure your evaluation of that is fair so that the price can be set accordingly.

Is there something that sets you apart, like a certification or license that others may not have? Take that into account. When I won an Emmy specifically for my editing, I knew that I could charge higher editing rates because I had the accolades to back up the price. If anyone says, "Man, your editing rates are a little steep," I can quickly respond with my experience to justify the cost.

Have you worked at several major companies and have valuable knowledge from those experiences? Take that into account.

I've sometimes heard people mention some of my past high-profile clients in conversations when I'm around.

"Yeah, he used to work for such and such, isn't that

cool?!" It can be a bit awkward for me, but I've learned to use that to my advantage.

When it's time to talk money, those people are more inclined to respect my price because they respect where I've been. It's not about bragging or name-dropping every chance you get, that would be obnoxious, and you may get the opposite reaction you're looking for. It's about making your résumé work for you. Everything you've done, every place you've been, and every client you've worked with matters. Take those things into account and make sure you accurately value your skills and experience.

On the other hand, if you are someone with less experience, make sure you aren't overestimating. It's not my intention to shoot down anybody's dreams, but you have to be realistic about where you are in your career. If you just graduated college or have only been on a couple of real jobs, be honest. Don't try to jump straight to the top of the charts just because you feel you're talented enough to do it. Talent is great, and I'm not saying you should lowball yourself if you haven't had the same opportunities as others. There just needs to be an honest evaluation of your experience.

This isn't a one-time thing either. You should make sure you account for your experience and skills as they grow. When I was working salaried jobs, I kept an eye on my abilities and my growing expertise to see how that impacted the opportunities around me. I was always looking to progress. If I changed jobs, I would always ask for more money from the next company, even for the same position. If I stayed within a company, I wanted to negotiate my salary at least yearly.

This wasn't motivated by greed. It was an understanding that as my skills and experience grew, it was only fitting that my compensation did as well.

AMERICA'S TEAM OR NOT, I NEED MY BREAD!

I had to put this idea into practice when I started working for the Dallas Cowboys.

During my interview process, things were going really well. They loved my work, and I was really interested in the opportunity. I was confident I'd get the job, but then things stalled. I didn't hear from them for a few weeks and was confused after feeling like I was a lock for the role.

When I finally reached out for an update, I was told that they did like me for the position but were hung up on my salary requests. They were aware of what I was making at my current job and were struggling with the fact that I was asking for nearly double.

At that point, I had two options: I could either fold and accept less than what I was asking for or stand firm on what I knew was a fair salary for my skills and experience, even if I wasn't getting that amount at my current job.

Understandably, many people would take less money in that scenario, given that it was such a big brand. If I had told people I took a significant pay cut in exchange for the opportunity to work for an NFL team like that, no one would think I was crazy.

People often stay stuck in a salary bracket because they don't think they can make the jump out of it. They might feel that it's impossible to make any significant moves to the next level without changing positions or some major event like getting another degree or certification. Whenever they receive any sort of pushback about it from a company or client, they assume the client is right, and they are wrong. In my situation, I knew what I was asking for was fair. The company I was leaving was notoriously cheap and had refused to bump my salary up for four years, despite my skills and experience growing extensively. So it wasn't a matter of "If I should be making that amount." It was just about finding the right company that would value me and my work.

I decided to stand firm and bet on myself. I was confident that the price I was asking for was fair for my skills and experience. After some minimal negotiations, I got the job with the desired salary. Because I understood my value and was able to remain confident about it, I not only got what I was asking for, but I set the tone for my time there. I always felt like people respected me in that building, and I genuinely believe it was because of how I handled my salary negotiations. When you respect your value and others can see that clearly, they have no choice but to respect it as well.

What about you? Is this something you're keeping in the forefront of your mind? When was the last time you increased your prices? When was the last time you asked to negotiate your pay? Now compare that with where your skills and experience lie compared to the previous year. How much have you grown and developed professionally?

Why should your skills, development, and growth trend upward while your pay stays the same? Investments are useless if there is no reasonable return.

TIME IS MONEY

Once you take stock of your experience and skills, you need to consider the time cost. This should be the most expensive part of you and the most significant factor in setting your value because it's a limited resource. You can get more money, buy more equipment, and build more buildings, but you can never get more time.

This is why I get frustrated when I see people giving their time away for free. Even if you are a beginner, there still needs to be a premium for the time you're spending on a project. Sometimes I see people advertising work that is at such a low cost that their pay equates to less than minimum wage when you look at the amount of time spent compared to what they charged. Is that truly the reality we want for ourselves?

Time is one of the most important things I think about when taking on projects and discussing prices. I'm not just thinking about the time it takes for me to film, edit, or deliver it, but everything involved in the project. This is where I see people leave a lot of money on the table.

Often, people are only thinking about the finished

project. They may think, *This is just a quick graphic I need to make,* neglecting the fact that they may have to do research for two hours to get the particular art style down or find the necessary elements. Sure, when it's all said and done, they may have only spent an hour in Photoshop, but they just gifted the client two hours of their time for free

Or people may say, "This is just a quick thirty-second video," and think it's simple, neglecting the fact that they have to spend hours doing preproduction, storyboards, and finding music. It may take a couple of hours to shoot and edit, but they just worked six-plus hours and only accurately got paid for two.

Usually, when a person felt as though they were underpaid for a job or project, they neglected to truly estimate the time and skill the task required. We've all been told by a client, "This should be simple," and then it ended up being the opposite. Make sure you get all the details you need to price out each project confidently. Use opening conversations with your clients to ask the right questions and really dig into what they are asking for. Clients often think big picture; it's up to you to sort out the details. Be realistic about your time and make sure you are being compensated fairly for the whole amount, not just the parts the client can see.

PREMIUM BENEFITS

In business, there's a saying, "Everybody wants it to be good, fast, and cheap, but you can only choose two. If it's fast and cheap, it ain't good. If it's good and fast, it ain't cheap."

Performance matters a lot! Just because you may be able to get something done in half the time as others, that does not mean that you should charge less for your time. If anything, it means you should charge more! As you work for people, you aren't just giving the time necessary for that particular project. You are giving the time you have already spent learning and becoming well-versed in your field. As the Jim Rohn quote at the beginning of the chapter says, "You don't get paid for the hour. You get paid for the value you bring to the hour."

You've worked hard to be skilled enough to handle this project quickly and efficiently, and that should be priced as a premium benefit for your clients.

LET'S TALK NUMBERS

Hopefully, you are starting to get a better idea of what you should be considering when setting a price for yourself. But you still might not know what the exact numbers are. Here comes the part you've been waiting for!

As I said before, it gets tricky because there is no correct answer, and it can be confusing trying to figure out where to start. For some, a rate of fifty dollars per hour may be fair, while for other occupations, that figure may be low. This is where you have to learn to do research and understand how the market you operate in can give you an idea of the exact numbers you should be landing on.

I'll sometimes tell this to people when they ask me for advice on their prices and I can see the look of disappointment on their face. They may think, *Really? That's it? An internet search? That's your groundbreaking information?*

It's really that simple! It's just like when a sports player signs a contract. Their agent has done research and put together comparisons for players with similar stats to see what their client should be making and uses that to negotiate. They could ask for a little more or less depending on certain factors, but the baseline for their number comes from looking at the market.

By taking into account the things we talked about like skill level and experience, you can easily talk to others and search online to see what the exact numbers should be for your situation. Some of the things I searched for when I was putting together my prices were things like:

- "Freelance videographer rates in Texas"
- "Video editor rates based on experience"
- "Hourly rates for professional video producers"

These searches will produce the numbers for any position, based on any amount of experience, and in any geographical location. Now you see why I needed to get you thinking about your own skills and experience before we could get into the numbers. When you research this information, it should be easy to plug in your own personal details and land on your price.

PLAYING THE MARKET

People can sometimes feel like this process should be more complicated. They think about how hard it has been to set their prices and really can't believe the answer is that simple. It is because the market dictates majority of the numbers. I can confidently communicate my price to potential clients because I've done my research and I know that what I'm charging is fair in my industry based on my skill level and experience.

But for me to have that trust in the system, the market has to remain balanced. That is why I stressed the importance of finding comparisons based on your personal skill level and experience. If you're a professional with years in the game, a lot of money invested, and a cultivated set of skills, you should not compare yourself to someone with less professional experience. And vice versa, if someone is less experienced, they should be realistic about their rates compared to where they currently are in their career. This is not only a priority for helping you set your own value; it's essential for the market's stability.

IT'S BIGGER THAN YOU

It is not my intention to tell anybody how to run their business or handle their finances, but there's a good chance that if you're neglecting these market values, it could be affecting others.

Take the stock market as an example. There are layers of rules and regulations for a reason. If you could do whatever you wanted, whenever you wanted, chaos would ensue as the scales become unbalanced. They even sent Martha Stewart to jail for messing with the system. Why do they take it so seriously? Because the stability of the market and everybody's money depends on it.

Pricing work is no different. There needs to be a balance. Unfortunately, I've seen people dangerously tip the scales in both directions.

Someone who should have a much higher rate is charging so much less. Perhaps it's because their business is slow, they have free time and need the extra money, or they really want to work with a particular client, so they lower their price in hopes of getting the gig. They discount themselves to seem more appealing.

The client ends up getting amazing work but the price was super cheap. When the next person comes goes to work with that client, it's hard to stand on experience and value with a higher rate because they expect comparable work for half the price.

On the other hand, someone with less experience might set their prices really low or even do free work because they haven't built up their confidence yet. Clients will start to expect free or cheap work from everybody, no matter the skill or experience level.

Playing this game on either side is dangerous, no matter the reason. Situations like this further propel the ignorance surrounding how certain professions should be paid and hurt the market for everyone else.

SET IT AND STAND ON IT

It never bothers me when someone tells me that my prices are high because I've done the research to know that it is fair within the market. If they were to contact anyone else with my level of experience, that person would likely quote them the exact same price or close to it.

When a project falls through, it's natural to try to analyze what went wrong. People begin to wonder what they could have done differently to get a better outcome, and usually, price is the first thing that comes to mind. They think, *Maybe if I came in at a lower price or cut my cost in half, the client would have worked with me.*

These thoughts are even more intense as you first send out higher prices. Resist the urge to backtrack and discount yourself. I'm at peace any time someone declines my services due to my cost being out of their budget. Sometimes people are cheap, and other times they honestly just cannot afford it. Either way, I know that I am presenting fair rates for what I bring to the table.

A quick note about the market: Do your research and consider what you find, but don't allow it to be the only information you use when setting your price. For example, I used to get emails from Glassdoor about the average salary for a video producer in Dallas. My last salaried job was triple the amount they calculated!

I'm not trying to brag or stunt on people. Many factors can contribute to the gap. I've increased my rates by winning major awards for my work, adding high-level clients to my résumé, and having access to more advanced equipment. All of those things translate to better quality and experience for my clients. Take into account that the average gives you a baseline but should not be your only source of info in setting your prices.

Whatever number you come up with, set it and stick to it. In later chapters, we'll discuss when and how you should offer discounted rates, but for now, you need to figure out what your services are worth and get comfortable presenting that number.

HOURLY RATES VS DAY RATES

Once you find a basis for how much your time and skill set is worth, being able to plug the numbers in is simple. Some people choose to work using day rates; others prefer to charge by the hour. If you want to find your half-day rate, multiply your hourly rate by six, and if you want to calculate your full-day rate, multiply that hourly rate by ten. Make sure you're charging overtime too! My hourly rate goes up when I'm asked to put a rush on a project, work longer than ten hours in a day, or work outside of regular business hours. For example, I once had a shoot where someone asked me to take some photos and videos in a recording studio overnight. I was able to charge them a little more due to the odd hours.

These tools should help you be more comfortable setting a rate for your time. But that's not the only price you should present to a client. As you'll see in the next chapter, you have to start thinking about more than just your personal time when it comes to your work. What about the cost of doing business?

Things to Remember

- Break the negative self-talk, you're worth your price! (No more imposter syndrome!)
- It's your job to set your value. Don't allow anyone to have that power over you.
- Use internet searches and conversations with others in your field to get a feel for what you should be charging based on your personal details and use those numbers to put together an hourly rate and a day rate for your services.
- Be realistic as you do your research. Find numbers comparable to your skill and experience level.

---

1. Clance PR, Imes SA. The imposter phenomenon in high achieving women: Dynamics and therapeutic intervention. Group Dyn. 1978;15(3):241-247. doi:10.1037/h0086006
2. Bloom, Ester. "Only Half of Job Seekers Negotiate, but Those Who Do Usually Succeed." *CNBC*, CNBC, 24 May 2017, https://www.cnbc.com/2017/05/24/only-half-of-job-seekers-negotiate-but-those-who-do-usually-succeed.html.

CHAPTER 2

IT TAKES MONEY TO MAKE MONEY

" *I'm not a businessman, I'm a business, man.*

Shawn "Jay-Z" Carter, Rapper and Entrepreneur

One of the biggest mistakes many people make when setting their price is neglecting to account for the cost to do business. They may have the details figured out regarding what to charge for their time, but they aren't incorporating the expenses of managing a business. Even if you are just one person freelancing, you should still view yourself as a company and understand that it costs money to keep the lights on. The operating costs vary depending on the industry but include purchasing equipment, taxes, insurance, and hiring others to help get the job done. If you aren't accounting for any of these expenses when setting your prices, you likely aren't recouping any investments, and you might be losing money.

As a video production company, I own tens of thousands of dollars worth of equipment. On top of that

IT TAKES MONEY TO MAKE MONEY

upfront cost, I have monthly expenses such as media storage, editing software, music and graphic licensing, mileage and gas, laptops, cell phones, high-speed internet service for fast transfers, and electricity.

These are just a few of the operating costs I have. What are some of yours? Or maybe you haven't given much thought to it. Take a second to make a quick list of all the expenses in your line of work. It doesn't have to be every exact dollar being spent. I just want you to begin to think about these things and how much money is going out.

The cost of operation directly impacts the price of the final product. As you spend more to raise quality, the cost should increase.

There is a reason why a Mercedes-Benz costs more than a Toyota Corolla. Sure, the brand name has something to do with it, but it's really about features. Mercedes-Benz can charge more because their features will blow Toyota out of the water. That Mercedes will come equipped with massaging leather seats, automatic windshield wipers, high-end technology packages, and many other things that will make driving that car a much better experience. Additional features come with a price.

What does this look like in your own business or work life? If you are constantly upgrading your equipment or the tools you use to do your job, are you making sure your rates reflect this? This is an added benefit to your clients and therefore needs to be incorporated into your pricing model.

However, this isn't an opportunity to start passing off

every penny to the people you are working with. You don't want to nickel and dime anyone. Your client should not be footing the bill for things that are not benefiting them. If you choose to buy a new camera comparable to your old system, that's not a good reason to justify a cost increase to your clients. If your old laptop worked just fine, but you decided to buy a new one because Apple won't stop making the same computers with different names, it's not up to your clients to pay for that. Make sure you aren't tacking on extra fees without reason every time you spend money on your business. Try to think about the benefit it presents to the client. Then you can confidently have a conversation with them about why there may be a cost increase, or the price may be higher than others in your same field.

When I purchased a RED camera, a more than twenty-thousand dollar camera system, my rates went up. Clients would often ask what was so special about it and why did shooting on this camera cost more? When I told them it was the same camera used on many feature films, usually the questions stopped there. People understood paying a premium price for a premium product, and they were happy to access that level of quality. You have to be prepared to explain the benefits of the tools you use to do your job if they come with a cost.

It's okay if you don't have access to the most up-to-date equipment or twenty-thousand-dollar cameras. Still, make sure you're finding a way to recoup your investment in business expenses.

THE COST OF DOING BUSINESS

There can be a long list of expenses you should consider when putting together our price. However, there are two that I see people skip over all the time:

• *Equipment rates* — Every time you use your equipment, whether it be a laptop, a camera, lights, etc., you are putting wear and tear on it. Eventually, that equipment will break or become outdated, and you will have to buy new equipment to continue to work. How do you plan on replacing that equipment? If you aren't charging clients to use your equipment, you could be putting yourself in a bad position when it's time to fix or upgrade outdated equipment. This also applies to the equipment you don't own and may have to rent as well. Whether it be a day rate or a fee rolled into the final budget, your rates should include the cost of equipment usage.

• *Hiring subcontractors*— The other cost I see creatives and businesses overlook is hiring subcontractors. You may not always be able to pull off every job alone. Maybe as a graphic designer, you need to hire an illustrator to help complete a particular aspect of the project. Perhaps you need to hire an assistant or a second shooter as a photographer. Maybe you have to hire an editor or an extra set of eyes as a writer. Whatever it is, this is something else that is often added to my proposals to clients. However, many people only think about their own rate and end up having to pay subcontractors out of their own pockets.

This is another reason why asking the right questions during your initial conversation with potential clients is essential. You must fully understand what the project entails to bring in the right people or equipment. The last thing you want to do is tell a client you can do a project and only account for your rate, finding out later you may need to bring in others or rent some equipment to help it along. Now you're faced with either going back to the client to ask for more money or eating the cost yourself. Make sure you're thinking about who and what each job might require and budget accordingly. Without the proper understanding of the recipe, you can't go shopping for the right ingredients.

Be prepared to explain the reasoning behind these costs too. If you're hiring people, renting a specific location or equipment, or adding some other expense, don't be surprised if the client starts asking questions if they are looking for places to cut the budget. It's common to hear things like, "Do we really need to hire this person or be at this location? We can save a little bit of money if we cut it." You need to be ready to explain the value that these added costs bring and how the project may be affected without them.

THINK OF YOURSELF AS A CORPORATION

I had a photographer friend who I was helping put together a proposal for a restaurant menu redesign. She was brought on to do the photography, but then the restaurant owners decided to toss her the whole project of designing the menu. She was now in a tough predicament, trying to figure out how she could handle the photography and a massive graphic design project in the short time window that the client was asking.

She was wondering about the optics of hiring another person since the client asked her to do the work. It's not unusual for clients to try to lump services together, especially in the creative world. Some assume that you must know how to take photos, shoot videos, create graphic designs, and everything else because all the roles bleed together. And they may ask you for all of the above, thinking it's much cheaper since you're a one-stop-shop.

You have to draw the boundary lines. While I am a photographer and videographer, I rarely accept projects where the client asks for both from me. I figure out in which role I will be able to best contribute to this project, and I hire out for the other.

I explained to my friend that she needed to hire someone for the graphic design portion of the job and charge a fee for her role as a project manager. That last part is key! I see many people only account for the cost of the person they're hiring. Remember, you have to account for all of your time on a project. Finding a graphic designer, writing out emails, having meetings to explain the project's progress, and playing mediator between the client and the designer would all be time spent that she should be compensated for.

How might you have handled that situation? Would you have taken on both roles and stressed yourself to get it done? Or would you have tried to bring on some help but would be too afraid to ask the client for a larger budget, so you take a loss?

I've handled it both ways before, and neither is ideal. Trying to wear every hat on a project leads to subpar work because you can't focus on doing one thing well. That also leads to burnout and frustration. And trying to hire out with no budget causes you to make pennies for your time. You and your business will end up in the red. Money will be coming in, but not enough to make a profit.

My buddy Cam broke it down to me the best way I've heard it. We talked about this concept, and he told me, "You have to think of yourself as a corporation, not an individual." Not only is Cam a great designer and photographer, but his advice is also on point! I don't care if it's just you in your home office getting things done; if you want your business or work to grow exponentially, you have to start thinking about the bigger picture. It can no longer be you on a solo mission to save the world. Hire some help, rent some equipment, bring in the tools you need, and don't be afraid to ask your clients to pay for it. The final product will be better, ultimately leading to bigger clients and projects.

WAIT TO GIVE OUT A NUMBER

Depending on your field, it can be intimidating trying to understand all of the associated costs. Begin to familiarize yourself with the rates of others in your industry and the equipment you may have to rent regularly to quickly have a ballpark idea of the budget you'll need for each project.

However, I make it a habit to not give any numbers upfront when a client is asking. We've all had those situations where a client is giving you the idea and pressing you for a price. Politely decline to answer or to even give a ballpark number. I do this often, especially when hiring out or renting equipment. I need time to contact others, find out their rates and availability, and calculate an accurate estimate.

If a client is pushing for an answer immediately, simply tell them, "Hey, let me run the numbers and see what it will cost. Give me a day to gather some info, and I can send you a full proposal by email." They may not like it, but it allows you to think about everything you need to make an informed decision. It also prevents you from giving a number that may be unrealistic, which can cause disappointment and frustration for the client if the final price ends up being higher.

UNCLE SAM GOTTA GET HIS CUT

Another sneaky expense is taxes. As a freelancer or business owner, it's up to you to handle your taxes. You should be setting aside at least fifteen to twenty percent of your income to go towards taxes. Otherwise, you could end up with a surprise bill that might be tough to pay at the end of the year.

Not only should you be saving for your taxes, but also keep track of everything you can write off as deductions. I write off EVERYTHING. Any equipment I purchase, gas and mileage, even my cell phone and internet bills get added to help cut my tax bill. Most of those expenses I mentioned can be used as tax write-offs. Make sure you claim every dollar spent to maximize your profits.

Are you starting to see how quickly all these things can add up? Some of you may be even reading this thinking, *I need to double or triple my rates!* If you are, that's good! That means the information is being downloaded the right way. It's not about charging more just because you can. It's about thinking about all the ways money goes out of your business to maximize the money coming in.

Things to Remember

- Always be aware of the money you are spending on your business or career, and make sure you have a plan to recoup those investments!
- Think of yourself as a corporation! Think of ways to view your work beyond yourself. You may have to hire subcontractors, rent a location or equipment, or put out money to make money. Don't eat those costs. Pass them off!
- Don't rush to give out a number when someone contacts you to do work. Take the

time to accurately calculate the numbers. Don't take too long though, as that can be a turn-off for some clients.
- Don't forget to set aside money for taxes! Be sure to keep track of all your expenses so you can use them as deductions!

CHAPTER 3

IT'S NOT WHAT YOU SELL, IT'S HOW YOU SELL IT

> *I've seen great salespeople sell the crap out of bad stuff, and I've seen people with no sales skills undersell good stuff.*
>
> *Kerry Lofton*

Now that you know how to price yourself and add up the cost of doing business, the most challenging part for many people is making the ask.

It's one thing to sit down and come up with a rate you feel you deserve. Standing firm and presenting that price to the client requires a different kind of confidence.

Notice I didn't say <u>ask</u> for your price. I said <u>present</u> your price. In looking at it as if you are asking someone to pay your fee, you further reinforce the idea that you don't deserve it. As a result, you may believe that people are doing you a favor by paying you when it is just a fair exchange for your work.

We need to break that mindset. It's not a matter of arrogance; it's more about confidence. I appreciate any time a client accepts my proposal, pays me fairly and trusts me to take on a project. I couldn't do what I do without the fantastic clients who believe in me and make the investment in my business. However, the price is the price. Therefore, I'm not asking for validation when I present it.

I'm always exuding confidence when presenting my price, down to the smallest detail. I remember when I realized I needed to change how I was wording my communication with clients. When I first started sending out larger quotes, and I was still uncomfortable, I would always end my emails with, "Let me know what you think." That statement seems harmless, but that was a subtle way of my insecurity about my prices showing up. What I was really saying by that was, "Here's my price. Are you okay with me charging that? If not, let me know, and I can cut it down. I probably won't even put up a fight." When you open that can of worms, the client could have a list of questions about your prices because you may come off as hesitant. And if you have doubts, they'll have doubts.

Now, I send my emails with a different tone. I say something along the lines of: "Hey, attached is a copy of the proposed budget and a deck with all the ideas I'd love to create for your company. Let me know if you have any questions, and if not, I can go ahead and get a contract and the invoice for a deposit over."

I keep it short and sweet. I still allow them to ask questions, but it comes off as confidence. I'm not exposing my budget to unnecessary doubt because I asked the client to validate it. I'm being helpful but stern, letting them know that I'm firm on my price.

When you go to a restaurant, the prices on the menu are not suggestions, nor are they asking for your approval to charge that amount. The server never presents the menu and says, "The filet mignon costs seventy dollars. Is that okay?" I can promise you that the restaurant owner isn't in the back saying, "What did they say when you gave them the menu? Did they think the prices were too high? Maybe we should discount it for them because I don't want them to leave!" They are showing you what they have to offer and how much it costs, and you can choose to order it or not.

Often, whether a client decides to work with you is not about the price you are charging. It's about how you present it. Instead of being bold and confident, are you timid and second-guessing yourself? That fosters questions about the validity of the pricing you have set. The client may feel like you're just throwing a number out there, and there's no reason for them to respect it. It could also bring up questions in the client's mind as to whether you can handle the project. If they can sense that something is off during the money talk, it may turn them off to working with you altogether.

When you lack confidence in one area, it always bleeds into others. People can feel those things when you're presenting your price—and that matters. A whole lot!

A LUXURY EXPERIENCE

Using that same restaurant example, let me ask you: How would you feel if you sat down to eat at a high-end steak house and the menu was presented to you written down on a napkin? It's poorly done in crayon, words are misspelled, and the napkin has stains. If this was a hood spot, you might overlook it. But it's not! It's a fancy place that you had to get all dressed up for, and the steaks cost one hundred dollars. You'd expect more, right? Despite how great the food might be, that initial impression might be enough to make you get up, walk out, and go to another establishment. The presentation should reflect the cost.

It's the same principle when you present your price to a client. You may not be writing on napkins with a crayon, but are you making sure your presentation is solid?

When you send a client a budget, how are you presenting yourself and your services? Do you just drop a price in an email or a text message? Or even an informal phone call?

"Hey, this project will cost you ten thousand dollars. Sound good? Great! Send me a check!"

That might work with smaller projects where people Venmo you a couple of hundred bucks here and there, but good luck getting anybody to handle bigger budgets that way.

The way you present your service is just as important as the service itself. I've seen great salespeople sell the crap out of bad stuff, and I've seen people with no sales skills undersell good stuff. It's about presenting value, the experience of getting to work with you, and making your clients understand why they should pay the price you're asking. You don't want to be the person who has so much to offer the world but is hindered because you can't confidently and accurately articulate it.

Let's look at ways you can present your price professionally and confidently. Throw away the napkin with crayon on it, and let's level up!

PUTTING TOGETHER A PROFESSIONAL PROPOSAL AND BUDGET

Step one is learning how to put together professional budgets and proposals. This process differs from person to person, but all that matters is that you put actual numbers and thoughts down on paper. Some people use spreadsheet software like Numbers or Microsoft Excel. Others use online services. Some use PowerPoint to put together whole decks with pictures, examples, and a full breakdown of how the project will go from start to finish. Whatever you choose to use doesn't matter as much as how the final product looks.

It needs to be clear and concise. You don't want to send a fifty-page PDF that the client must sift through to determine how much you're asking them to pay. But you also don't want it so simple that it seems like you just opened a word document and typed a number in.

In my own business, I use a combination of Microsoft Excel and a website called Milanote.

I start with Milanote, which helps visualize and organize my ideas. I love that there are a ton of templates to help you get started on whatever you're working on. These boards save me a ton of time when I'm putting together a pitch to a client, especially if the client hasn't fully agreed to the scope of work just yet.

Often, I have to create these decks to get the client to even agree to work together before we can get to discussing numbers. Because of that, there are instances where I spend valuable time putting a deck together, only to have the client ignore it or choose not to use my services.

In a way, I'm working for free. But the time investment is well worth it to be able to confidently and professionally present my ideas.

Those couple of hours spent organizing your thoughts into a visually pleasing format for the client can be the difference between them catching the vision completely and feeling confident about investing in your services or choosing to go another route. I've even had people comment on how professional my pitches were and how that played a role in them wanting to work with me!

First impressions are everything. People see the level of quality in a proposal or pitch deck and assume that the same high level of effort will translate to the actual work being done.

Once I organize my ideas visually, I use an extension for Excel called TrueBudget. Where Milanote is used to lay out my ideas, TrueBudget gets into the details of what it costs to make it happen. It's an empty spreadsheet with line items for everything you could ever need to charge for, and all you have to do is plug in the numbers.

When I first started doing budgets, I'd open up a

blank template and just look at all the things that were options to charge for, and I would then research how and what I should be charging for those items. TrueBudget was a great resource when I had no idea what a good starting point was.

Once you plug in your numbers, it calculates the total cost and exports a PDF you can send to the client. This gives them a final number for the project and a line-by-line breakdown of where every penny goes.

And while this is great for presenting your budget to the client and helping them understand the numbers, it can be a blessing and a burden.

THE DANGERS OF COST TRANSPARENCY

Allowing a client to see every single number can be a double-edged sword. On the one hand, knowing where the money is being spent can help make them more comfortable with larger budgets. On the other hand, there are likely things they won't understand about how you end up at a specific price for your work and begin to nitpick every cost.

When you go to McDonald's, you don't have to know that a beef patty costs seventy-five cents, a slice of cheese costs twenty-five cents, and the bun costs fifty cents to get to the three dollars and fifty cents you're paying for your burger. You order the food, they tell you the price, and it's that unspoken understanding that it's based fairly on what it costs to make and allows McDonald's to also make a profit. You can't protest the price and then demand that the manager show you how much every element of that burger costs to know that you're being charged fairly.

The same is true for business. In your respective field, you are the expert. You know your business costs and how much above that cost you have to charge to make a profit. The client won't always understand the reasoning behind these costs, nor should they. You're the professional, and there is a reason why they hired you.

This is where trust comes in and the importance of running an honest and upstanding business. You can't use this as an opportunity to overcharge anyone because they don't know any better. I've seen people run their businesses this way, and though they seem to get ahead, it never works out for them in the long run. Great client relationships are built on trust, and I believe people can always sense when they are being taken advantage of. Maybe not right away, but it will definitely sour relationships in the long run.

It's tempting to feel frustrated when a client asks questions about numbers. Some people's knee-jerk reaction is to assume they aren't seeing the value and are trying to be cheap. And while this can be true at times, it's not always the case. Making sure a client understands where their hard-earned money is going is important in building a trusting relationship with you and increases the chances of your proposal being accepted. I don't expect my clients to understand what goes into production. However, it is my job to make sure they know that every penny spent is being translated into something that will ultimately help achieve their vision. Many deals don't go down, not because the numbers weren't right, but because the value wasn't adequately communicated. If a client can't afford my fees, I want them to be disappointed because they're missing out on the experience of working with me, not relieved because they think they dodged a bullet because the numbers seemed shady.

IT DOESN'T HAVE TO BE WEIRD

I remember when I sat down to discuss my retainer fee when I started doing work for Demarcus Ware. He could tell that I was really uncomfortable, and he said something that rings in my head every time I'm talking money: "It doesn't have to be weird, man!"

He wasn't being rude or mean; he was offering me amazing advice. Presenting and standing on your price doesn't have to be weird or feel dirty. It's actually healthy to have these conversations to reinforce your own value while also educating the client.

I just wrapped up a project for a major company where I had to defend my price. It was a massive project that required travel, several days of shooting, equipment rentals, location scouts, and several rounds of editing. After asking questions to get a gist of the project's requirements, I put together the budget and sent it over. The client came back almost immediately to say it was much higher than expected. I didn't panic because I knew I had followed my steps and had accurately quoted them based on the scope of work. Remember how I said earlier not to be swayed by a client's reaction to your budget?

I politely offered this company an opportunity to speak with me over the phone so I could offer some clarity. It's okay to have these open conversations. You have every right to walk away when people are undervaluing you, but you should always allow the opportunity for conversations to be had about these things.

Their questions were about a couple of items on the budget they had never heard of before. Things such as "preproduction days," which are the hours spent working before a shoot ever happens. Or "travel days," which is the charged rate when more than four hours are spent traveling. They weren't saying they didn't want to pay me for those items; they just wanted some clarity on where their money was going.

I explained to the client how much time I would spend on Zoom calls and meetings to gather the details, write out shot lists, rent equipment, pick up supplies, prep cameras to make sure everything was in working order, and more. When the conversation was over, the client realized how much I was doing and felt like the preproduction costs were more than fair.

Instead of being frustrated or discouraged by their questions, I used that opportunity to bring them deeper into the process. This conversation allowed them to have some peace about investing in the project. It also helped pave the way for a better understanding of what some of these things truly cost. We are currently in talks about the next project, and the conversations about budgets are so much easier because I took the time to educate them. Just because someone may be asking questions about your price, this may not mean they don't intend to pay you. They may just need clarity.

There are different views on this among different people. Some believe that the price is what it is, and clients can take it or leave it. Others feel they need to explain every detail to the client; otherwise, they may miss out on business.

I fly somewhere in the middle. I believe there needs to be transparency, particularly for new client relationships, to build that trust. Having a professional budget probably saved me from losing that project from the example I just gave. Had the client just seen a number that was too big for them, they might've just walked away. But being able to see every line and ask questions and understand made them more comfortable with stretching their budget.

However, it's a fine line between educating and begging for the budget to do the job we are asked to do. I'll redirect the conversation if I feel like a client is asking questions to try to penny-pinch, and there is no trust there. If it gets to a certain point where every little detail is questioned, I will sometimes decline the project depending on the vibes I'm feeling. If there is no trust before the money is spent, the rest of the project won't get any easier. Just as clients have the right to decide if they want to work with you, you have the right to turn down projects.

In a perfect world, you'd send out your lovely, professionally made proposal and budget, and the client would accept it, write you a blank check, and everybody would live happily ever after. Unfortunately, it rarely happens that way. Negotiations can and will happen, and the dreaded conversations about getting it done for cheaper will ultimately arise.

Don't fret, though. There's a way to handle it!

Things to Remember

- Don't think of it as asking people to pay your price; consider it as presenting. Break the mindset that people are doing you a favor when they pay you fairly for your work.
- Don't slack on the presentation! How you present your ideas and budgets matters! Putting together a professional proposal can be the difference between gaining a client or missing out on work.
- Be transparent and answer questions, but don't beg! It's okay to pull the curtain back for your client to be more comfortable with your prices but don't allow them to nitpick every cost if it affects the budget you need to do your job.

NEGOTIATING YOUR PRICE IS NOT WRONG; IT JUST NEEDS TO BE DONE IN THE RIGHT CONTEXT.

JUST AS THE SAME FIRE THAT CAN PROVIDE COMFORT AND WARMTH CAN BURN A HOUSE DOWN IF IT IS MISUSED, NEGOTIATIONS AND DISCOUNTS CAN EITHER HELP OR HURT YOUR CAREER DEPENDING ON THE CONTEXT.

CHAPTER 4

YOU GOTTA BE WILLING TO NEGOTIATE

> *Money is the goal but oftentimes in order to get it, you have to retrain your brain to value experience.*
>
> *Curtis "50 Cent" Jackson, Rapper and Entrepreneur*

I understand that so far, it can seem like I'm coming off as inflexible when it comes to my rates. We've spent so much time talking about money and how to make more of it that it might seem like that's all I care about, and it's all I want you to care about. However, that is not the heart of my message. The truth about this process is that there will still be times when you might accept less than you may be worth or have to negotiate your price. That's okay!

Don't worry. We aren't tearing down what we spent so much time in this book to build. Negotiating isn't the enemy; it's a chess piece that you should use to your advantage.

Sometimes people can become so jaded about all the wrong clients that took advantage of them that they resolve to never accept less than they're worth again. I get that frustration and mindset, but it's dangerous.

Being unwilling to negotiate in the right situation can cause you to miss out on valuable opportunities and investments that can help build your business and take it to the next level. Negotiating your price is not wrong; it needs to be done in the proper context. Just as the same fire that can provide warmth and comfort can burn down a house if it is misused, negotiations and discounts can be instrumental to your career or harmful, depending on the context.

So let's talk about when is the right time for these situations.

LEARNING WHEN TO GIVE DISCOUNTS

When it comes to discounts, one of the things I mainly avoid is "bulk discounts." This is where a client tries to justify paying you less in exchange for the promise of more work in the future. The fact of the matter is, your time is your time. It's the one thing you provide that you cannot ever get back. You can recoup financial investments and buy new equipment, but you can never get your time back. Therefore, a premium must be charged for it.

I recently had a conversation with someone who asked for half off my rate using that bulk discount logic. Their defense was, "Well, I'd really love to do more work with you in the future and put you on a monthly retainer. If you give me a price break now, we could do more together down the line."

While I understand their line of thinking, it's a horrible deal for my business. My time is not something I feel comfortable discounting in bulk. That works for toilet paper at Costco, but not for me. Furthermore, if a person does not honor my time in small quantities, why would I allow them to devalue me on a larger scale? If a client cannot offer me the professional respect to pay my worth for one hour, the last thing I want to do is give them more of my time at a discounted rate. When I start to sense the person I'm dealing with has this line of thinking, I usually run the other way.

However, this is not to say that all discounts are wrong or if someone is asking about them, you have to cut them off. Sometimes it is not their intention to be cheap or rude. Working with many small businesses, especially during the recent pandemic, and watching how it has impacted our communities, I realized that some companies are trying to do the best they can with the budget they have. I consider a lot of these things when deciding when and where I give price breaks. But discounts have to be mutually beneficial for BOTH parties!

It can be challenging trying to decide when it is the appropriate time to give a discount. Here are some questions I ask myself as I'm considering it.

"How much is this client making on a particular project and how much is their company worth?"

If I'm working with a significant client or corporation with access to bigger budgets, I have to think long and hard about why they may be asking for a discount and then decide based on the information I find. It's not about "pocket watching," but you have to be aware of the companies and businesses you are dealing with. You might be more apt to give discounts to a small, local business before you cut your prices for a major brand that probably has the budget to pay you, but they are being cheap.

That was also one of the reasons I decided to stand firm on my salary request with the Cowboys. Maybe I would've been more flexible with a little league team but not one of the most valuable sports franchises in the world.

"How long have I known and worked with this client?"

I usually try to reserve discounts for my most loyal clients. There's something to be said about continuing to build a relationship on successful work and trust. Out of appreciation for a company valuing me and the work I do, there are times when I may offer discounted rates or toss in a couple of free assets in the interest of taking care of those who take care of me.

When offering discounts to new clients, you risk losing out on money with no plan of getting it back if they only decide to work with you once.

"What am I getting in return for the money I'm losing out on by discounting my rates?"

Asking myself this question is how I usually avoid the trap of offering discounts in exchange for exposure or social media promotion. I see so many people getting caught up in this, especially younger creatives or newer business owners. They are unsure of what lies ahead and are usually not in a position to let money walk out the door, so they are more inclined to give out discounted rates to these companies, hoping that the exposure will lead to more business. They would rather receive half of what they are worth rather than nothing.

If this is common practice for you, I hate to shatter your dreams, but it's a facade. These scenarios rarely work out in favor of the person doing the free or discounted work. Exposure can't pay bills.

I've been in situations with clients who have hundreds of thousands of followers, and they have posted my work on social media, tagged me, and made sure to put my name out there to all those people. Does it lead to more exposure? Sometimes it does. I may have gained some followers here and there, but it rarely leads to any money in my pocket. And if by chance someone does contact me, I still have to do more work to get paid.

And even then, you better hope that the old client didn't go yapping to their friends about how you're the person who will do free work in exchange for a tag on Instagram. What do you think the new client will be inclined to do? Will they be eager to pay your rate? Or will they want the hook-up price like their buddy?

Good luck getting out of that loop. You risk creating a stream of ungrateful, non-paying clients. If you don't value your time, don't expect anybody else to respect it.

The same goes for bigger companies that want to allow you to work for them at a discounted rate just because of the name on the building. These companies can sometimes take advantage of the fact that they're a big name or brand and treat the job as if it's a privilege to work with them. Resist the urge to discount yourself just to rub shoulders with them.

The truth they don't want you to realize is that they need you more than you need them. That's so counterintuitive to the lie that has been perpetuated. That breaks the belief that you should bow down and be thankful that you can get into the presence of a particular company. It's a myth. You don't have to discount yourself to be worthy of working for them. If your work is good enough to be on their radar, it should be good enough for them to pay your full rate.

Those were just a few examples of some scenarios where it's pretty easy for me to say no to a discount request. I'm not saying that discounts should never happen. You should be flexible when the right opportunities present themselves. Don't be so set on getting every dollar you can that you miss out on opportunities to network, invest, and potentially build something worth much more.

I can speak from experience that there are things worth more than money. Let me tell you a couple of stories about how this has helped propel my own business.

The first example is a client who had a minimal budget for a project I was asked to work on. The project was moving quickly, and they already had the concept and the budget locked in when they contacted me. In this situation, somebody with no knowledge of production decided to set the price for a project they knew nothing about. They underestimated the time and cost of the project, and the price they offered reflected that.

Nonetheless, I prayed about the opportunity and decided to take it. It was a large company that I knew could afford a bigger budget, and they were also well aware of the value I brought to the table, but I decided not to fight it. We did the project, and it was a great success, despite me barely making any profit off it.

If the story ended here, I would look like a fool. All investments involve some element of risk, but I'm always confident betting on myself. The gamble I took paid off when the company contacted me a couple months later for a project with a much higher budget.

The quality I gave them on the first project was one factor, but my attitude and the experience I brought to the set played a significant role. During the first project, I was very strategic, making sure I was having the right conversations with the right people to let them know how much of a discount they were getting and what the actual cost of the project should have been.

Instead of complaining that I was underpaid, I gently educated and explained the process. The client felt like they were learning, not being belittled because they were cheap. They were surprised to learn the actual cost of my services and felt appreciation because I showed up with such a great attitude despite being extremely underpaid.

For the second project, I presented the budget I felt was fair and necessary to complete it. The budget was accepted at nearly ten times the amount I had been paid for the first project. That situation actually set me up enough financially to be able to take the month off to write this book. That's a return on an investment anyone would be happy with!

It's not always about what you get paid upfront. It's about strategically building a relationship for more business in the future.

HAVE A VISION BEYOND JUST GETTING PAID

Curtis "50 Cent" Jackson speaks about the idea of accepting less money for a better opportunity in his book, *Hustle Harder, Hustle Smarter*. I actually had a chance to meet him in Los Angeles a few weeks ago. Instead of asking for a picture, I pushed past his entourage just to get an opportunity to look him in the eye and personally thank him for sharing this valuable nugget. This one piece of advice has been one of the most effective strategies I use in business.

In the book, he tells how the hit TV Show *Power* ended up being his least lucrative deal at first. When he signed on for the first season, his goal wasn't to get a major payday; it was to get a major opportunity. He took an enormous pay cut to be involved, an amount that he could've made elsewhere for much less work. But he had the vision for a much bigger plan. What he sacrificed in pay was returned to him with interest as he inked a 150 million dollar deal with Starz after the success of the first season of the show.

He attributes that win to humbling himself to be able to work at a discounted rate and play the long game to reach his goals.[1]

Everything you do for your business daily puts you

in a position for the next big project or client. Don't despise the small beginnings if you can see a way to make it work for your benefit in the future.

USE BIG FISH TO CATCH BIGGER FISH

If there is an opportunity for the final product to be a great asset for me in the future, I'm more inclined to work within a smaller budget. It's important to note that these situations are done on my terms. I never allow a company to come in and sell me a dream. I decide based on the vision I have for my business.

For my second example, I had a company contact me about a project for an event surrounding their foundation. It was for a major celebrity, and I had this grand idea for a way to tell the story of the work and the impact that this foundation had on the community. I went big on my proposal to impress this client, and it worked. It was completely different from what they expected, but they loved it. There was only one problem—the idea, and therefore the budget was much bigger than they anticipated. It wasn't about being cheap, either. As a foundation, they literally didn't have the budget to make it happen, no matter how much they loved the idea or trusted in my abilities.

At this point, I could give them the smaller video they originally asked for that worked within their budget, or I could swing for the bigger idea knowing I wouldn't have the budget I'd hoped to get. By doing so, I would still offer this company my original vision but I would eat the costs of the larger production.

I ended up rolling with the bigger idea. Though I took less in payment, there are a couple of essential things to understand:

- I didn't work for free. I still received compensation for my time, and though it was less than I initially hoped for, it still allowed me to sustain my business. It also set the right expectation for the client. They understood that there was a significant gap in what they were getting versus what they were paying. They appreciated the extra care I took to make the project great and build trust with them. They also understood that it is still a working relationship and that I expected fair compensation. I didn't become the guy who will do free work for them because of who they are. In fact, I recently had a conversation with someone within the company who told me, "Don't ever worry about what you're charging us, we'll always make room in our budget for you!" That's a far cry from our initial conversations where the budget was tight. The seed I planted grew into a client who respects my work and price.
- There was a clear goal for the discount to be mutually beneficial to both parties. So many times when companies are asking for discounts there are no clear terms on how it will benefit both parties. On my end, it was a

unique opportunity to work on a project and bring a fresh vision to a particular industry I wanted to break into. I knew that because of who the project was for, it would bring attention and connections to my business that would be worth more than the money I missed out on. And for the company, it was an opportunity to have access to a higher level of production to present to their stakeholders and begin asking for bigger budgets to allow projects like this to become more doable in the future.

If a company is asking for a discount and the only reasoning behind it is for them to save money, you have to think long and hard about honoring it. If you really want to work for that company and they don't have the budget, try to think of creative ways for it to benefit you. There has to be some give and take. Otherwise, somebody is being taken advantage of.

You can present cheaper options. Maybe you can't swing for the major idea, but you can do something on a smaller scale. This allows you to still be paid fairly for the work, build a relationship with the client, and you don't have to undervalue yourself in the process.

You don't have to be so rigid that you don't ever accept a penny less than you're worth. I promise you'll get nowhere fast because money isn't the only thing that matters. Connections, networking, investments, and opportunities play a major role in advancing your career. You just have to keep these things in the proper context and always have a plan and process for negotiating your value.

- Discounts are not wrong, they just need to be done in the proper context. It must be a mutually beneficial situation!
- Being unwilling to negotiate could cause you to miss out on valuable opportunities and connections to help your business grow.
- Have a plan for the situations where you choose to discount your prices. Don't let a client sell you a dream about more work or social media exposure. Count the costs and make sure it is a wise investment!

---

1. Jackson, Curtis. *Hustle Harder, Hustle Smarter*. Amistad, an Imprint of HarperCollins Publishers, 2021.

THERE IS MORE AT STAKE THAN A BIG PAYDAY.

THE MONEY COMES AS AN ADDED BONUS, BUT CONFIDENCE IS THE GOAL.

CONFIDENCE TAKES YOU SO MUCH FURTHER THAN MONEY EVER COULD!

CHAPTER 5

WHAT YOU DO WITH IT IS UP TO YOU

> "It's not easy, but it's simple."
>
> *Dr. Eric Thomas, Motivational speaker*

There's nothing left to do but to apply this information. Knowledge without application is useless. A seed in your hand holds all the potential in the world but can yield no fruit if it isn't planted and watered. There's more at stake here than just a big payday. The money comes as an added bonus, but confidence is the goal! Confidence takes you so much further than money ever could.

As I said at the very beginning of this book, I kept it short because the information is crucial. If you made it this far, you now have that information. What you do with it is up to you. You may not have the golden answer, but you have a dang good set of tools to start with and build upon.

I'm still learning and growing myself every day in my business dealings. I don't have a Harvard Business School degree—or any degree, being a college dropout—

but I have experience. I have proof that it works. You can have the same experiences if you just jump out and do it.

To plant a seed, you have to get your hands dirty and have faith. You need faith that knows that when the seed is in the ground, and you can't see it, the process is still going strong. It may take months of work before you see the tiniest sprout protruding from the soil. Resist the urge to stop doing the work when you don't see immediate results.

Some of you will try the things we discussed in this book and find that it's easier said than done. Clients might meet you with some resistance as you step into a new way of doing things. You might hear feedback about how high your prices are, or you may price yourself out of clients you're used to working with, so the work could slow down. You might even have more people than usual tell you no when you send your rates to them.

I've dealt with it all. Don't give up and go back to the old way of undervaluing yourself and your work. Don't bend just to make a dollar. Stay the course. Market to different clients. Revisit the info and see where you can better communicate the value so that people understand it and want to pay your price. Like I said in the first chapter, the responsibility belongs to us!

Whatever you do, make a promise that you won't go back to undervaluing yourself or allowing the world to discount you based on insecurity ever again. As I said before, I can accept a discount when it has a business strategy attached to it, but never when it's done out of fear.

Kill that spirit of fear now and step boldly into your new future!

FREE GAME

While this book was mainly focused on the pricing aspect of business and freelancing, I realize that there are a lot of other topics and things people may have questions about. Whether you're a new or seasoned business owner or freelancer, sometimes it can feel like we're all just trying to figure it out.

I'll sometimes ask questions to my mentors when I feel like I don't know what's going on or where to start, and I'm relieved to know they're taking it as they go, just like I am.

So while I can't cram everything into this book, I didn't want to leave you without some other tips and best practices for business. This is a quick-fire list of some of the things I've learned that can hopefully be helpful to you on your journey. Enjoy the free game!

ONE STEP BACK, TWO STEPS FORWARD

Sometimes you have to take one step back to take two steps forward. I see many people turning down opportunities they feel are beneath them. The path to the top will not always be a straight line. You could be missing out on valuable opportunities to learn, network, and strengthen your career.

Ninety-five percent of my work involves me directing and being in a leadership role. I've been in the game for more than eleven years, and I've worked hard to be in these positions. However, a few months ago, I took a job as a production assistant on a set for a Walmart commercial. If you aren't familiar with roles on set, while a production assistant sounds cool, it's basically a glorified coffee collector. It's also one of the lowest-paid jobs on set.

But I took the opportunity with great joy and have no regrets. I met great people, built some lasting connections, and further weaved my way into a world I am trying to become more immersed in. Sometimes you may be the big fish in a small pond. Other times you're a goldfish in an ocean. Embrace every single moment and learn from it!

ALWAYS HAVE CONTRACTS IN PLACE

———

No matter how small the amount, always have some sort of written contract or agreement for the work being done. This can be tough for last-minute projects or things that move quickly, but it's crucial. People end up not wanting to pay or dragging their feet at the end of a project much more often than you think. Ensure you're protecting yourself by having a contract that thoroughly communicates what work is being delivered and what compensation has been agreed upon.

JACK OF ALL TRADES, MASTER OF NONE

———

Just because you know how to do multiple jobs doesn't mean that you should. I'm skeptical about accepting projects where I have to wear multiple hats. Especially with creatives, people assume that you can do it all, and a lot of times, we can. But there's no reason for you to be the photographer, videographer, graphic designer, marketing director, and social media coordinator all in one role. Trying to focus on too many things hinders the quality of your work. Only focus on what you do best. Offer help and support in those areas where you can, but don't allow yourself to own those roles.

CHARGE LATE FEES

Charge late fees on your invoice and discuss this with the client upfront. The amount can vary based on the industry and the amount of time that goes by before the invoice is paid. Figure out what works for you. Be aware that many bigger companies are net thirty, forty-five, sixty, or even ninety. This means that you should expect payment within thirty days, forty-five days, sixty days, or ninety days. Sounds crazy, right? I've heard horror stories of people getting checks in the mail three months after a project was done. Feels super unfair when we're pressured to deliver under tight deadlines and then have to wait for weeks or months for payment, but it's the lay of the land. Discuss how the company handles payment ahead of time and try to negotiate a quicker payout if you need to. While you cannot charge late fees before the time a company has set as their net, you can charge late fees on time past it.

GET HALF OF YA' BREAD UPFRONT

Get deposits as often as you can. Depending on how fast a project comes together, people often forego deposits. No matter how fast things move, push to get one on every project. This provides you the upfront capital if you need to hire contractors, book travel arrangements, rent equipment, or purchase any other tools necessary for the project. It also gives your client some skin in the game. They're less likely to bail on the project or drag their feet on it when they have something invested upfront.

I once had a client make me pay for all my travel out of pocket and then took three months to pay me. It was very trash.

UNDERPROMISE, OVERDELIVER

Resist the urge to try to accommodate people on less than realistic deadlines. As your business grows, you won't be able to keep up with promising to deliver things on shorter timelines. Underpromise and overdeliver.

I do two to three weeks for videos, depending on the project and my schedule. If I get it done earlier, great! If not, I'm not stressing myself out or causing a bad experience for the client by having to push back my promised delivery date.

EVERYBODY EATS

Don't be afraid to pass off work to others. So much of my work has come from other videographers passing off projects they didn't have time for or weren't the right fit for, so I do the same. When we build other creatives up, it builds the community up as well. Don't be stingy, and don't be afraid to put somebody else onto a job.

TIERED PRICING

Give pricing options and packages. Clients are much more likely to work with you if they have multiple pricing options to choose from. Provide high-end, mid-level, and low-budget options. Be sure to communicate the differences in the final product for each level so the client understands where the extra money is going for every option.

YOU DON'T NEED A NEW CAMERA

Resist the urge to invest in more equipment for the sake of it. Your investments play a part in dictating the cost of your work. If your current setup benefits your clients just fine, don't invest in more expensive equipment that will add more expenses with minimal value-added.

TAKE BREAKS OFTEN

Feels like I need to list this one ten times for most creatives. Don't let yourself get caught up on the hamster wheel, going on and on until you've earned yourself a VIP ticket to burnout. The "grind 24/7" culture that exists is really unhealthy and frightening. Listen to your brain, and take one when you need a break. You'll actually be more productive than if you just try to power through.

And if you're working for a company that encourages this sort of culture, start updating your résumé!

SAY NO... A LOT!

No money is better than stressful money. That may sound privileged, but be careful that you aren't saying yes to everything, especially if you are only doing it to get paid. I know many people who make bank but are too stressed to enjoy the fruits of their labor. If the vibes feel off, or if you just aren't a good fit for a project, don't be afraid to say no and pass it off. That added stress will only hinder your creativity and affect the other tasks you could be doing that you are passionate about.

Clients can choose whether they want to work with us. We have the right to decide if we're going to work with them.

TAKE 'EM TO COURT

I pray you never have to deal with a client who refuses to pay. But if you find yourself in that situation, don't fight it in your own strength. I recently found out how easy it is to file a suit in small claims court. Depending on your city, it can be done online in less than fifteen minutes. You can even have the local sheriff show up to the job, business, or home of whoever is refusing to pay up for a small fee.

Here's the best part: most times, you won't even have to go through with the whole process. For most people, being hit with a summons to go to court is enough to get them to give in and pay.

WHEN THEY GO LEFT, YOU GO UP

One of the reasons my career was so successful at the Dallas Cowboys was because of my ability to think outside the box. One of the ways I did this was refusing to look at sports content for inspiration, although that seemed logical. Instead, I pulled ideas from movies, TV shows, and music videos and brought them into the sports world. Several new content ideas came from that process, and my work stood out because of it.

Whatever field you're in, find ways to go against the grain. Do what everybody else is not doing. It can feel awkward at first, but you'll eventually start to stand out from the crowd.

Extra Resources

Budgeting software: www.truebudget.io

Storyboarding, scheduling, and planning: www.milanote.com

Contracts, invoices, and keeping track of business expenses: www.HelloBonsai.com | Use the following link for a free month: https://www.hellobonsai.com/invite?fp_ref=kerrylofton

There are tons of other resources, examples, and info out there. This book isn't a comprehensive list by any means. Always be out to learn, grow, and seek more information to improve your craft. Let every day bring you a lesson that you can apply to your life and business. That's how I've been able to thrive with no formal schooling or training. I've just been blessed by God with a gift and a mindset to get out there and do it!

    I pray many blessings on your journey as you confidently put a value on yourself and your garden grows!

About the Author

Kerry Lofton is an award-winning video producer, photographer and entrepreneur. He lives in Dallas, TX with his wife, Bri.

After dropping out of college in 2011, he taught himself videography and photography. Since then, his journey has allowed him to film and create work for companies such as the Dallas Cowboys, NFL Films, AT&T and several other major brands and celebrities.

Not only does he love creating and telling stories, but through writing, consulting, and mentorship, he also has a passion for helping others reach their full potential and understand their God-given purpose.

twitter.com/KerryLofton
instagram.com/KerryLofton

Made in the USA
Columbia, SC
11 April 2022